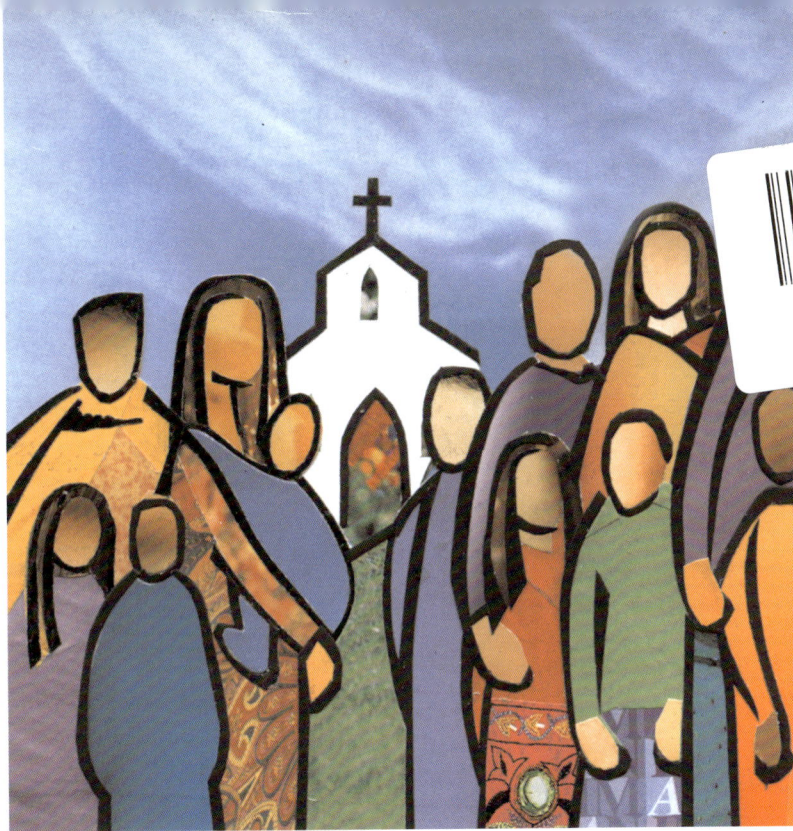

Faith builder

a basic guide on how to live as a Christian today

a redemptorist publication

"What do we do now?"

"How do we keep growing in our faith?"

These are questions that we often get asked at the end of a Parish Mission or Retreat. Indeed, they are the questions which faithful Christians ask throughout their lives. In "Faith Builder" we offer you a series of reflections which will help you to grow in faith, hope and love.

We begin with the place of the Church's liturgy in our life – especially the celebration of the Eucharist. Then we look at how we make decisions and act morally in Christ. Continuing our reflections we look to the Teaching Church to give us wisdom in facing some of the crucial areas of modern living, money, relationships, etc. Finally, we explore what is involved in being a member of the Church today.

You will find space throughout the book to write down your own thoughts and reflections. However, you may also find it useful to share with other members of your community about the various topics. Existing faith-sharing groups may also like to use these as they seek to discover how to live the Christian life fully.

Our prayer for you, as you read these articles and reflect upon your life in Christ, is that the Father

"May give you the power through his Spirit for your hidden self to grow strong, so that Christ may live in your hearts through faith, and then, planted in love and built on love, you will with all the saints have strength to grasp the breadth and the length, the height and the depth; until, knowing the love of Christ, which is beyond all knowledge, you are filled with the utter fullness of God. Glory be to him whose power, working in us, can do infinitely more than we can ask or imagine; glory be to him from generation to generation in the Church and in Christ Jesus for ever and ever. Amen." (Eph 3.16-21)

Richard Hagen, C.Ss.R, Joe O'Connell, C.Ss.R. and Ian Kane, C.Ss.R.

contents

A gathering

A group of visitors were staying near to an old parish church in an inner city area. Finding the church closed, they went to the presbytery where they found a warm welcome from an elderly priest, who was living in the house in retirement. The priest offered to show the visitors around. They were shocked by what they saw. All signs of Christian devotion were gone from the building. The altar, the lectern, the tabernacle were gone. The benches were no more. The echo of emptiness filled the place. The priest shared his thoughts with the visitors. Not so long ago the building would come alive every Sunday in what was a lively multi-cultural parish. The people, he said, had made this building special. Now they were all gone. It had been a vibrant parish in its day but as a result of local redevelopment the people had long moved out and their houses demolished. Without the people, said the priest, it had lost its purpose and usefulness.

A building is just a building, but a family makes a home. God's family gathers at God's behest every Sunday to worship and to grow in love. There are many beautiful church buildings, but it is people who make them come alive. The church in which we worship is the house of God for the family of God. The people come before the building, however magnificent. Gathering happens when we allow the Holy Spirit, who has touched our hearts, to draw us in to the table of the Lord to be nourished and united. We stream to the house of God that he might strengthen the bonds of love among us. Just to gather together is an act of worship because all hearts are focussed on the Father who loves us.

notes

_____

_____

_____

_____

_____

_____

_____

_____

_____

_____

No Carbon Copies

We are not identical in our feelings or expectations as we gather for the Eucharist. We are the assembly of God and a very mixed bunch we are. There are no carbon copies here. In this great gathering we are blessed by the rich variety of personalities and characters. While all are made in the image of God, each is unique. Our unity is found in the Lord who calls us friends and who wants to share his life with us. In the great assembly we thank God for one another.

The Holy Spirit

He stood among them and gave them his peace. This is how Luke depicts the Risen Christ in company with his disciples. Jesus stands in the midst of the assembly of his disciples to teach them and to prepare them for mission. This moment is captured in the final chapter of Luke's gospel. The disciples are in Jerusalem and Jesus instructs them to wait for what the Father has promised, namely, the outpouring of the Holy Spirit. On Pentecost day the Spirit comes down and they are changed forever. They are loved, and they know it. The joy of the Spirit gives them strength. In the Spirit they lead others to Jesus. In our gathering for the Eucharist the same Holy Spirit is poured out upon us to make us one and to make us strong.

Action Plan

Is there someone in the parish whom you know and has not been to the Eucharist for a long time? Why not share with them the thoughts in this article? Your gentle courage may be their lifeline. Remember, the Holy Spirit is in you.

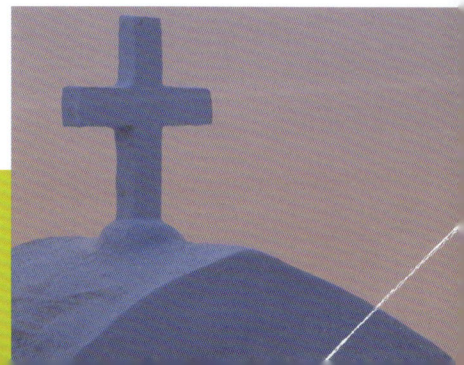

Praise

The baptism was arranged for Sunday afternoon. Invitations had gone out to a wide circle of family and friends. There would be a party after the service. Most of those invited had already met the baby and all loved her to bits. The baby was beautiful and had been the focus of ceaseless conversation before her baptism. "She has her father's eyes." "Her mother's features are very evident just below the nose." She brought out the best in all who saw her. On that Sunday deep appreciation engulfed the family and their guests. The celebrations gave a lift to their faith on that joyful afternoon as they gave thanks to God for the gift of this child.

It is also possible to give praise in time of difficulty and sorrow. Edward had retired early because of painful arthritis. He had always been fit and active and his work had taken him round the world. Life had been full. His affliction arrived quickly and with little warning. There were days of deep despondency, but Edward's faith was strong. He had discovered the power of praise as he cultivated the habit of thanking God for everything in his daily life. His favourite phrase sums up his attitude: "God is good and I count my blessings."

The Purpose of praise during Mass

The positive gives us strength and builds up our self-confidence. We can see beyond the immediate problem that confronts us. In our Christian tradition there is a piece of advice that takes us beyond counting our blessings. That advice is: 'Praise the Lord'. We know from the Eucharist that it is right to give God thanks and praise. We begin the Mass by praising God at the Kyrie and the Gloria. This should be done in song to give it fullest expression. United voices in united praise. Praising God frees us to give ourselves wholeheartedly to him in the celebration of our Eucharist. Praise brings to our agitated minds a state of peace because we are focussed on the giver of peace. In that gentler frame of mind we can bring our deepest desires to the Lord who cares for us. The power of praise softens us and helps us to hear the gentle voice of God addressing our anxieties. Through praise we find a way forward.

From the Bible

The story of the Ten Lepers is familiar one to us. The incident is recorded for us in the seventeenth chapter of Saint Luke's gospel. Jesus is on his way to Jerusalem to fulfil his mission. On the way ten men suffering from a dreaded skin disease confront him. Their disease has isolated them from their families and communities. In response to their pleading he instructs them to go to the leaders of their communities, and on their way all are cured. Understandably they would rush back to their families and be restored to human society. But one of them becomes aware of the enormity of the blessing given him. He is overcome with gratitude and cannot contain himself. Praise and thanksgiving pour from his heart as he acknowledges the gift. This man showed himself open to the deepest healing of all. He had turned to God in sickness and in health. He remembered God through thanksgiving and praise.

Action Plan

Think of one joy and one sorrow that you have experienced during the course of your life. Praise God for both.. Use the 'Gloria' from the Mass or your own words. Do this over several days.

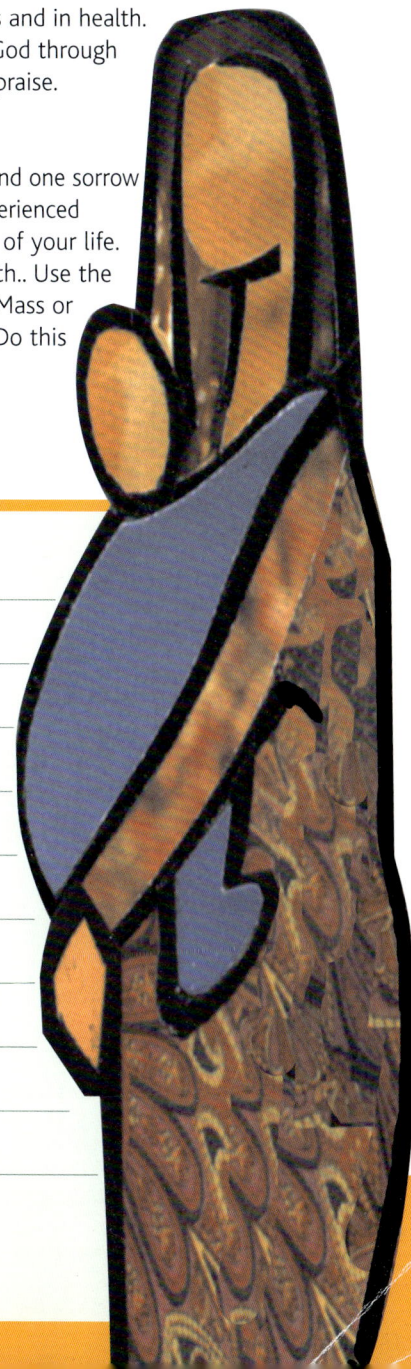

notes

_____

_____

_____

_____

_____

_____

_____

_____

_____

Receiving God's word

"Please speak up, I can't hear you!" To be hard of hearing is a very frustrating experience. It makes communication such a struggle for those who suffer from it. We take it for granted when we can hear well because we take it as natural. We may not always like what we hear, but we like to hear. But of course we are not limited to the physical act of hearing with our ears. We live in a visual society where image is important. Billboards are cleverly designed to catch the eye and convey a message quickly and effectively. People judge what they see and whom they see. We watch for facial expressions or folded arms and wonder why this person appears defensive. We are expert at receiving information. We read letters, postcards, e-mail, and timetables. We devour newspapers and magazines. We hunger for information and news. For millions the regular evening news is a must. We listen carefully with our minds.

notes

_____

_____

_____

_____

_____

_____

_____

_____

Receiving God's word at Mass

We have a duty to receive God's word through hearing and reading. As surely as we need to receive the Lord Jesus in Holy Communion, we need to receive God's word. Attentive listening will bring its rewards. Our faith grows through hearing the word of God. We believe that the power of the word of God is so great that it is the energy and support of God's people. Our longing for news through the mass media is a sign of a natural desire to know. The most important knowledge we can have is knowledge of God. Perhaps we feel too distracted to listen to the readings. We may have young children with us, clamouring for our attention. The tiredness of the past week may finally be catching up with us. The sound system in the church may be poor and we just give up trying to listen. In all these distracting situations we need something to fall back on. That something is private reading of the Bible. In particular we prepare ourselves well for the Liturgy of the Word by spending time during the week with next Sunday's readings. Our familiarity with them gives us greater concentration no matter what distraction comes at us. Be familiar with God's word.

Example from the Bible

Samuel was God's gift. His mother, Hannah, had no doubt about it. In gratitude she dedicated him to the service of God in the Temple. The boy was apprenticed to Eli the elderly priest, who looked after him and guided him. This story is told in the First Book of Samuel, in the Bible. Samuel was still a boy when he heard the voice calling his name, "Samuel! Samuel".
He ran to Eli the priest to acknowledge the summons. For a second and a third time Samuel heard the voice call his name. By then the old priest knew it was the voice of God and told the boy how to respond. On the fourth occasion God stood by Samuel and called his name. Samuel responded by saying: "Speak, Lord; for your servant is listening"
We want to hear the voice of God.
We have his word in scripture.

Action Plan

As early in the week as possible get hold of the readings for next Sunday's Mass. Use a bible with good footnotes for this. Once each day, for about ten minutes, go through the readings until you are familiar with every word and its context.

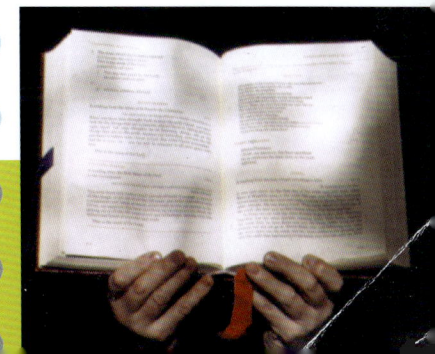

Doing the word of God

There is a story told of how St. Francis took a young novice with him into the town to preach the word of God. They walked around the market into the streets, passing people and stalls. Every now and again Francis would stop, listen to some people, talk to them, share a laugh with one or two, console and sympathise with others as they walked along. Eventually, without uttering a word, the saint and his by now confused novice returned home. "What about the preaching" the novice asked, "I thought you were going to preach?" Francis replied that the preaching had indeed been done. He went on to explain that we preach by our actions not by what we say. Perhaps it was to teach the novice or to preach the better kind of sermon that he did this. The greatest preaching is always that of example. "Be special," he said, "you may be the only Gospel your neighbour will ever read." A very simple message indeed. We preach the word of God by our lives, by putting the Word of God into action. [Hebrews 4:12]

Putting flesh on the words

The word of God has no effect on us unless we receive it into our hearts and respond to it. It is not just in hearing the word of God that we are changed. It is in doing the word of God. In the words of the apostle James, "Be doers of the word, and not merely hearers..." [James 1:22-25] It's easy to convince ourselves not to be "doers" of God's word. "I don't have time, I need to study the scriptures more so that I can understand them better, I am too young or I am too old. We fabricate many excuses to get away from our Christian responsibility of putting the Word of God into action. We convince ourselves that we're not able to "do" God's Word right now. We convince ourselves that we're not ready to witness, or teach, or lead in prayer, or take any sort of active role in bringing about God's kingdom. And so we come to Church each Sunday simply to hear the Word and remain unaffected by it. We remain as hearers of the Word but unconverted by it. We must put flesh on those words and so become doers of the word instead.

"The Word of God is something alive and active: it cuts like any double-edged sword but more finely." [Hebrews 4:12.]

"Be doers of the word, and not merely hearers..." [James 1:22-25]

The task of the Church

The task of the Church is not just to preach Christ to people, but to be Christ to people, especially to the poor and the suffering; we must become doers of the Word. We must proclaim the Gospels with our lives. The person in misery does not need a look that judges and criticises, but rather a comforting presence that brings peace, hope, and life. What our world needs today is a Church that can make the caring and compassionate Christ alive and real for a hurting and sceptical society. This responsibility is not for somebody else, if it is not for me, then it will be for nobody! Each of us has a vital part to play. We must take our Christian responsibility seriously. How can the forest be green unless the individual trees are green?

Our task

God desires for us to absorb His word into our hearts not just for ourselves to grow but for his Kingdom to flourish on earth. When we share the Gospel with others, the Holy Spirit can then help us translate God's word into everyday language that anyone can understand. This means that simply memorising the scriptures and quoting them at people is not what God is asking. It is the living word, not the quoted word, which changes people's lives. We must become that living word.

Action Plan

You must become the Gospels on legs, because you might be the only page of the Gospel a person sees today.

notes

_____

_____

_____

_____

_____

_____

_____

_____

_____

_____

Eucharist as gift

[Luke 22:19-20, 1 Corinthians 11:23-27]

As she lay in her hospital bed, ten-year-old Lisa Ostrovsky's (from Missouri, USA) thoughts were with a man she had never met. She said of him, "he is a friend who will help me and I love him for that." Lisa was given only months to live because she suffers from a genetic lung disorder. Ronald Johnson from England is the stranger who wants to save her life. He read about Lisa's plight in the London Jewish News. Under the headline 'Time is running out for Lisa' it told how the little girl needed new lungs and how her father had launched a global Internet search for a donor. Ronald responded to this plea and is to donate the lower part of one of his lungs, which will be transplanted into Lisa. Asked why he was doing it for someone he had never met, he simply said, "It is the greatest gift to give someone the chance of life".

The gift of the Eucharist

The Eucharist is the Church's most sacred treasure; it is a heavenly gift and is at the heart of our faith. It is intimately connected with the life of the Church and of all Christians. In the Eucharist Jesus gives us himself as spiritual food for our journey through this life. It is given so that we may have life through him. It enables him to remain with us forever. He did not abandon us but remains as gift under the form of bread and wine. Jesus first changed bread and wine into his Body and Blood at the Last Supper. In the Eucharist we celebrate the gift of our whole life – in it we celebrate Christ's love for his own church; his own creation – his body.

The liturgy of the Eucharist begins with the preparation of the gifts in which the bread and wine will be transformed into the body and blood of Christ. Receiving the gifts, the priest raises them and says a prayer based on an ancient Jewish Prayer, "Blessed are you, Lord, God of all creation..." This prayer reminds us that all we have and give comes as gift from God. In the Eucharist we become God's gift to others, channels of God's love to our world. It is not only the offering of the gifts of bread and wine but also the gift of ourselves. The bread and wine, symbols of our life and work, will be made holy so that we might be blessed so that others may share in this blessing. To fully celebrate Eucharist means partaking of Christ's life and Mission. Empowered by the Eucharist we become Eucharistic people – proclaiming the Gospel of love in simple practical ways. Our mission is to become the "Body of Christ" to our world.

New Life

Jesus tells us that we must eat his body and drink the chalice of his blood. His words are meant in the most literal sense. If we would accept his lifestyle and adopt it in the world, no child would ever again die of hunger, and no old person of loneliness. We would be attentive to each other, using the gifts we are to each other. We would become "the body and blood of Christ" for our world – what a gift!

A child who makes their First Holy Communion and indeed most people, feel special when they receive the 'body and blood of Christ'. For at the moment the host is received that person can say with St. Paul, "it is no longer I who live, but Christ who lives in me". That person who receives Christ is having a private audience with the Son of God. For the person who receives the Eucharist, there is the feeling of welcoming the Christ of the Eucharist into their heart. The Eucharist is the gift of a special friendship between God and us.

Action Plan

There is a saying today; "You are what you eat". In the Eucharist we are to become what we have celebrated – "The body and blood of Christ". Are we that gift to our brothers and sisters? Are we a gift that gives life for others?

notes

Eucharist as community

[Acts 2:42]

Recently I was in our local primary school. I asked a classroom of ten year olds, "Why should we go to Mass?" After various answers one little boy said very solemnly, "because Jesus told us to." From the earliest days the Christian community has come together to celebrate the Eucharist, or as we call it today, the Mass. The Acts of the Apostles, written around the year 70 AD, tells how the early Christian community gathered regularly for "the teaching of the apostles and the breaking of bread" (Acts 2:42). Today, 2000 years later, Christian communities still meet to celebrate the breaking of bread, and so remain faithful to those words of Jesus, "Do this in remembrance of me." From that night when Christ took bread and wine in his hands — and gave the apostles the privilege of being there and the power to change lifeless bread into the Bread of Life — from that night the world has never been the same.

notes

The Last Supper

The Last Supper wasn't a private pact Jesus established with individuals like the Apostles, Peter and John, the Pope or Mother Teresa. Although the Eucharist does come to us as individuals, it is however, more perfectly expressed as a community. When we come together, we come to share a meal, the Lord's Supper. There is little pleasure to be had in having a meal by oneself – especially if it's a celebration. It doesn't matter how exotic or good the food is, a meal is a natural celebration of people coming together. And so in the celebration of the Eucharist we come together to remember what Christ did – his compassion, his forgiveness, his healing, his teaching and ultimately his love for human beings.

Action Plan

Our relationship with God and more particularly the intimacy we have with God in the Eucharist has to be more than a one-to-one. It has to spill over into the lives we live with others. As Christians we are united by a bond so close that St. Paul called the Christian community, 'The body of Christ'. It is time we began to notice one another. Each person is a brother or a sister in Christ. Each person then must be recognised. Each person must be given some sign of friendship, be it only a smile, a kind word or a helping hand.

You are the Body of Christ,
and in the words of St. Teresa:

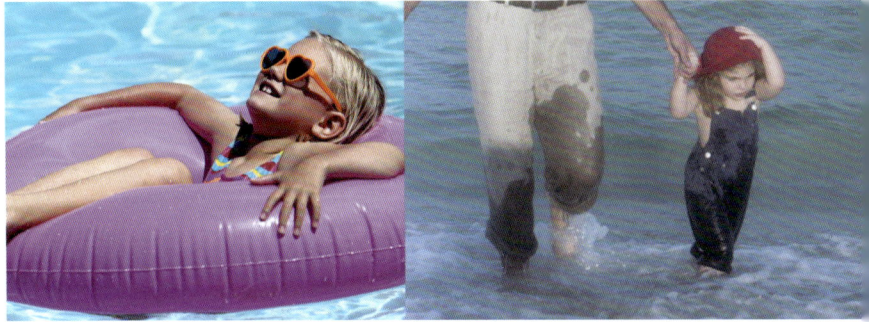

"Christ has no body on earth but yours;

No hands but yours;

No feet but yours;

Yours are the eyes

Through which he is to look out

with compassion to the world;

Yours are the feet

With which he is to go about doing good;

Yours are the hands with which he is to bless now."

The Mass is ended

It had not worked out quite as he had imagined it would. Just before his seventieth birthday Denis, husband and father of a large family, had informed the family that he knew all about their 'surprise' birthday dinner. However, he explained, he appreciated the thought and looked forward to the dinner just the same. The family had booked tables at a local restaurant and on the evening of his birthday treated him to the best. A close knit family, they wished the eldest son was present. He had spoken to his father by telephone that day for over an hour and sent greetings to the rest of the family. They knew he could not make it simply because he lived thousands of miles away on another continent. This was as close as they could get to one another. The meal was drawing to a close and the birthday cake was brought out. The bearer of the cake was the eldest son, who had secretly made the sacrifice to come for this event. Stunned silence was followed by tears and hugs and kisses. The experience of this celebration led them to a greater bond than ever before.

notes

_____

_____

_____

_____

_____

_____

_____

_____

_____

_____

Who is my neighbour?

For many people an inaudible sigh of relief greets the end of Mass. When the priest says, Go, they are glad to do so and abandon the building to its emptiness. For many others something very different happens. They linger in the church, glad to be together. There is no great rush to get out. Rather a warm spontaneous socialising takes place. People talk to each other and the atmosphere is pleasant. This latter group of people have grasped instinctively the importance of the end of Mass. It is not a dead or empty moment marking the boundary between church and real life.

It is the moment when all that has been celebrated by them in the Eucharist is gathered up and owned by them. Together

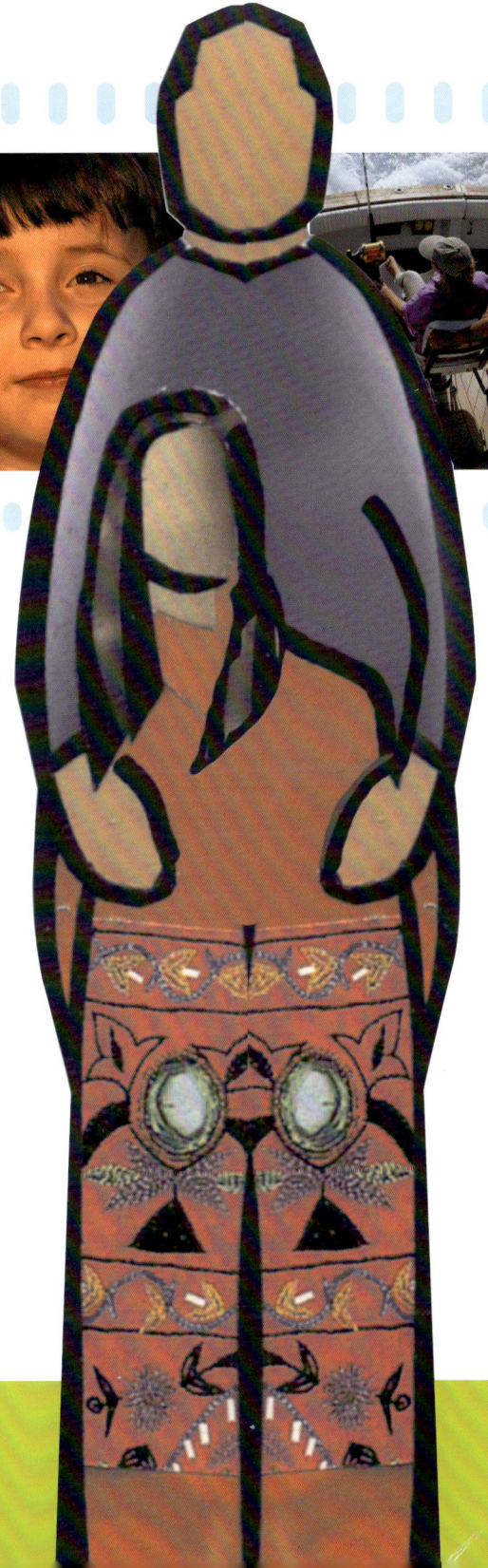

they have received the word of God and the Body and Blood of Christ. Instinctively they have accepted the Lord's gift of unity. They recognise each other as sister or brother and cherish the gift. They talk to each other, to the younger people, and to the children. For all there is the realisation that this experience of Eucharist has been very good. It is still good to be here together. They have grown in love and are ready to take the Gospel to others.

A simple story would clarify the answer. This is why Jesus told the parable of the Good Samaritan. This parable Is recorded for us in the tenth chapter of Luke's gospel in answer to the question, 'Who is my neighbour?'. The story is told to show that any and every person is my neighbour. It shows something just as important, namely, how do I treat my neighbour? The Samaritan translates his compassion into practical help. He bandages the man's wounds and takes him to safety. By the end of Mass, if we have truly opened ourselves to the Lord, we will have the caring compassion of Christ for one another. We will feel secure in one another's company. We will bandage each other's wounds.

Action Plan
At the end of Mass next Sunday speak to someone you have never spoken to before. It could be anyone of any age.

Sent to others

The strength of any team or group lies in the unity and commitment of its members. This is especially true of a parish community. Christ himself is our common focus and the bond of love among us. We belong together and we are strong together. The following incident highlights this truth. A famous evangelist was in conversation with a Christian layman who argued forcibly that he did not need to belong to any church. He felt quite strongly that he could be a servant of God without having to belong to any group.

The evangelist had other ideas. They had been sitting before an open fire. When the man had finished speaking the evangelist used a pair of tongs to remove a burning coal from the fire and placed it alone on the open hearth. while the other coals remained red hot together in the fire, the single coal soon fizzled out. Together we set the world on fire with the love of God.

The Lord sent us out

"Go in peace to love and serve the Lord." The Church's whole purpose on earth is to reveal to others the presence of Jesus. This parish is God's instrument for bringing the saving love of Christ into the whole world. It is a magnificent vocation given to us all. Strengthened by the Eucharist and purified by the word of God we go in the name and person of Christ to conduct his mission. Pope John Paul II has reminded us that the Church is universal in scope but that, in the parish, it finds its most immediate and visible expression. We are part of a worldwide fellowship introducing others to the love of Christ. As a parish community what will others see as they look at us? We have celebrated the Eucharist and need to ask ourselves this question: What improvements has it made to us as a community and as individuals? We must keep in mind that God always gives us what we need in faith to do his work. Over time others will notice the difference and begin to wonder about it. We can trust God to do this.

From the Bible

Fire touched his lips. This was the experience of the prophet Isaiah. His vocation comes to him in a dramatic fashion. We read about this in our bibles, in the sixth chapter of the Book of Isaiah. The prophet is granted a vision of God in holiness and glory. The sight is overwhelming and he plunges into despair. How can anyone so sinful see God and live? But God has a mission for Isaiah, namely, to proclaim the word of God to the people. In the vision God sends a red-hot coal from the altar to touch the prophet's lips. It is a symbolic purification to show Isaiah that he is now fit to do God's work. In our Eucharist something far more dramatic has happened. Our whole being has been touched by the fire of God's love. We have heard the voice of God in the readings and have received the Bread of Life from the altar. Like the prophet we now speak for God.

Action Plan

Join a faith-sharing group in your parish. This will train you for telling others about your faith.

notes

_____

_____

_____

_____

_____

_____

_____

_____

_____

The good life

THE ROBOT DO-GOODER: There was once a famous scientist who decided that he would create a robot that would do good and bring happiness to those whom it met. So he designed the right arm so that it would seek out opportunities to give alms to the needy. The left arm would reach out with a touch of comfort to those who were grieving or sad. The right leg would always run away from any sinful or evil situation. The left leg was made to find those who were in need of love and compassion.

"We are God's work of art, created in Christ Jesus to live the good life as from the beginning he had meant us to live it."

'(Ephesians 2:10)

When the scientist finished his magnificent robot he took it into town before switching on the power. Then he flicked the switch and the robot hummed into life. Nearby, a young woman was hunched over with an arm outstretched begging for money. The right arm seized its opportunity and instructed the rest of the robot to go to the young woman. But the left arm was aware of an old man sitting alone on a bench – his wife had died only days before and it wanted to head for the man to comfort him. The right leg wanted to flee the area as it was part of the sinful red-light district and, finally, the left leg wanted to head into the heart of the same area so that true love might be shown there. Before the scientist's eyes his robot whirled around and around before collapsing in a heap of tangled metal as it struggled to decide what to do.

notes

_____

_____

_____

_____

_____

_____

"For I tell you, if your virtue goes no deeper than that of the scribes and Pharisees, you will never get into the kingdom of heaven." (Matthew 5:20)

Doing Good or Being Good?

Have you ever felt yourself torn in many directions? Even though we may be committed to living good lives our problem is often deciding which good things we should do. We hear voices of other people – "this is what you should be doing". Our own inner voice often says – "you should do this good thing". And often the Church will point out things which we should be doing. How do we live a moral life without going crazy by being pulled in all directions?

"We are God's work of art, created in Christ Jesus to live the good life as from the beginning he had meant us to live it." (Ephesians 2:10) The key to living well is to live as a person formed in this truth – I am God's masterpiece. It is who we are that is more important than what we do. Everything we do will be illuminated by the kind of person which we are. God wants to form in us a character that will reflect Christ's love in each and every situation we encounter.

Action Point

Take time to reflect on the way you respond to situations and people. If you can make the time to write down your thoughts this will help you to see things more clearly. The following list of questions may help to focus your reflection.

• Do I really believe that God has created me marvellously and that I am God's work of art?

• When faced with a choice about what to do for the best how do I make my decision?

• Do I presume the best or the worst of other people?

• When other people do something which highlights a part of me which I don't like about myself am I gentle or harsh with them?

• Which situations do I avoid – why do I avoid them?

• What kind of person would I like to be?

Faith

OUR FIRST STEPS: In the beginning, a healthy baby simply lies at the centre of its own universe - food comes to it, hugs and kisses are presented on demand by the willing adults, and, for a while at least, everything revolves around this tiny infant. Gradually, as the child grows older, it begins to explore a little by shuffling around or by pulling things towards it. Eventually the baby begins to crawl with great expertise and can cause massive anxiety as it finds its ways into corners previously thought to be unreachable! In the end the baby switches from crawling to the magical stage of being a toddler - gradually becoming more and more confident in its ability to walk the stage of our world and make a difference to it.

Is there ever a time when the parents of a healthy young child doubt that their baby will learn to walk? It is assumed that, given time and encouragement, they will learn how to walk. Babies are taught to believe utterly that they can and will gain this miraculous talent for walking. The babies are determined to walk, the parents and brothers or sisters don't doubt that the baby will walk, and eventually the babies do walk.

notes

_____

_____

_____

_____

_____

_____

_____

_____

_____

Faith – Trusting our Relationship with God

As we make our way through life what is the rock on which we can base our life? What will make sense of, and bring meaning to, all that we are and all that we do? It is our firm conviction as followers of Jesus that it is our faith in God that is the foundation of our lives. The God of love that Jesus Christ reveals is certainly trustworthy – "It is not easy to die even for a good man – though of course for someone really worthy, a man might be prepared to die – but what proves that God loves us is that Christ died for us while we were still sinners." (Rom 5:8)

God is committed to us and has demonstrated the totality of that commitment in Jesus Christ, in his living, dying, and rising for us. There can be no doubting that God is on our side, that God has done everything possible to convince us that God has only good intentions towards us. It is this truth that will enable us to live our lives with confidence even in the very worst of times – whilst the world and the people surrounding us may not have our best interests at heart God's heart is overflowing with love and concern for each one of us.

Do you believe that God has destined you for greatness, for glory, for a life which brings healing, salvation, liberation to those around you? If this is not what we believe about ourselves then we have allowed alien voices to block this truth – God is the parent constantly encouraging us to move from shuffling, to crawling, to walking in the ways of love. Sadly, however, the influence of many of those around us can drown out God's words of encouragement and cause us to stay stuck when God is calling us forward, for " the glory of God is a human being fully alive" (Irenaeus).

Action Point

- Which people have been most influential (for good or bad) in my life so far?

- How have they each influenced my development (for good or bad)?

- How do I allow my relationship with God to influence the kind of person I am?

- What do I believe that God thinks about me?

- What can I do to deepen my relationship with God?

Hope

THE VISION OF LEONARDO DA VINCI: Everyone is familiar with the magnificent painting the "Mona Lisa". Its painter, Leonardo da Vinci, is widely admired as one of the giants of the artistic world. Yet, not only was he a giant among artists, his genius was also to influence generations of draftsmen, architects, sculptors and engineers. It seems that almost no area of human endeavour was allowed to pass him by. Not everything Leonardo designed worked as planned, not everything he started did he finish, yet it his immense imagination which still captivates us nearly five hundred years after his death.

How could Leonardo have imagined the flying machine and come up with designs (however unworkable at the time) only a few years after the printing press had been invented? Where did he get his inspiration for the flying machine? He took his observations of birds in flight and applied what he saw there to the challenge of getting people to fly. This gift of sight and observation is seen time and time again in his life and work – in observing the world around him Leonardo was able to imagine new possibilities and new strategies for a multitude of seemingly unrelated areas. The genius of Leonardo da Vinci was to truly observe the world around him yet look beyond to the possibilities that could emerge. This is the heart of hope.

Hope: Looking with the eyes of faith

"In a period of immense social, religious, and cultural upheaval, it is vital that there be a people who can look beyond the current reality and offer joy and hope to our needy world" (Vatican II – Gaudium et Spes – 1). It is with the eyes of faith that we can truly observe what is happening around us and yet still look forward to the reality of God's kingdom proclaimed in the person of Jesus Christ. Trusting in God's work of salvation accomplished in Jesus we can trust that God is leading the whole of history into the reality of the kingdom – a place, a time, an experience of God's liberating and uniting love for all people.

It is through this conviction of hope – that God has a plan for our human family – that we find the energy to undertake the sometimes arduous task of living the good life. Sadly, many Christians mistake a naive optimism (that "everything will be alright") without any basis for true Christian hope. Yet, true Christian hope is quite different – hope is the attitude of the believer who trusts in God's saving work in Jesus. The reason for our hope is the God who enters into our broken sinful world and shows us the way of true humanity – in this God has entered into an unbreakable covenant with us. Hope is the mind-set which allows us to live in today's world while striving forward with words and deeds which reveal God's kingdom of justice, peace and compassion.

Action Point

- Do I see myself as a hopeful person?

- When people are in need do I actually help them or am I content with offering words of hope and encouragement?

- Does my relationship with God, the teaching I have received, give me energy and enthusiasm for living with hope?

- When do I find myself most enthusiastic and energised?

- Can I learn from this and apply this zest for life to other areas?

notes

_____

_____

_____

_____

_____

_____

_____

_____

_____

_____

Love

IN THE COUNTRY OF THE BLIND THE ONE-EYED MAN IS KING... OR IS HE? In ancient times there were two small islands in the middle of the Mediterranean whose inhabitants were blind. They managed to live simply but contentedly. However, their lives were disturbed when two shipwrecked sailors were washed up on their shores, one on each island. The two shipwrecked brothers, Kakeus and Kaleus, were exhausted but recovered their strength after being cared for by the friendly inhabitants of the islands.

Needless to say both Kakeus and Kaleus discovered very quickly that the islanders were blind and that their own sight gave them tremendous advantages. Kakeus, being an ambitious man, began to enslave the islanders and forced them to build a large palace – from a large throne he ruled over them as a tyrant bringing misery and suffering to everyone on the island. Kaleus, however, began to see opportunities for helping the islanders to live safer and healthier lives. Spying healing plants growing up on the ledges of a steep cliff he would risk life and limb to collect them so that the infirm and the sick might get relief from their pain. He would warn the islanders of approaching storms and exhausted himself ensuring that everyone reached the safety of the village before the storms hit.

"If I have all the eloquence of men or of angels, but speak without love, I am simply a gong booming or a cymbal clashing..."

Love – opening up to God, self and others
"In the country of the blind, the one-eyed man is king." (Erasmus) But where does true kingship lie – in ruling or in serving? In what does our true greatness lie? In our ability to have power over other people or in our ability to serve other people? For the Christian the answer is very clear – an answer revealed in Christ who "did not cling to his equality with God but emptied himself to assume the condition of a slave." (Phil 2:6-7) At the heart of our desire to live the good life is the mystery of love. We are created in love, redeemed in love and sustained by the love of God – it is that same love which calls us to reach out with a servant heart to the people around us and beyond.

The primary challenge facing us as we seek to live out the Gospel in our daily lives is to cultivate a servant's heart, an attitude of mind that seeks not its own advantage but the good of those around us. Very often the Christian life can be caricatured as an easy way through life, as some form of a cop-out – however, the reality couldn't be more different. We see in giants like Martin Luther King, in Ghandi, and countless others, the true price of a loving heart.

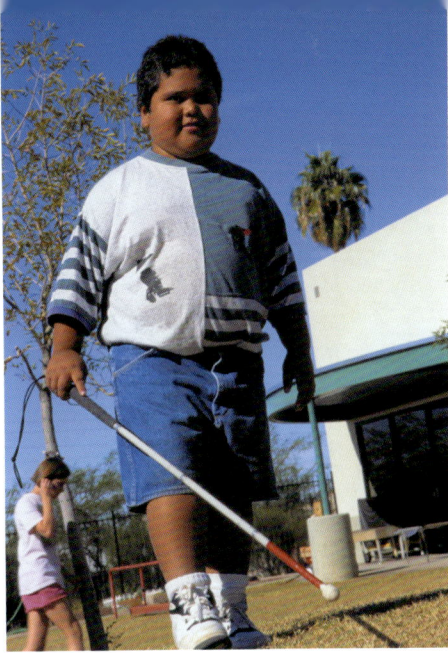

Action Point

Take time to reflect and pray about this passage from St Paul's first letter to the Corinthians (Chapter 13).

"If I have all the eloquence of men or of angels, but speak without love, I am simply a gong booming or a cymbal clashing. If I have the gift of prophecy, understanding all the mysteries there are, and knowing everything, and if I have faith in all its fulness to move mountains, but without love, then I am nothing at all. If I give away all that I possess, piece by piece, and if I even let them take my body to burn it, but am without love, it will do me no good whatever... In short, there are three things that last: faith, hope and love; and the greatest of these is love."

THE THEOLOGICAL VIRTUES

Central to the lives of all Christians are the three Theological Virtues, Faith, Hope and Love.

Faith: trusting in God's loving nature and believing that we are called into a relationship with God.

Hope: looking beyond the world we see and seeking to build up God's reign on earth.

Love: choosing to be like God in pouring out our lives for others.

notes

29

Prudence

CHOOSING LIFE: There is a very striking image of a donkey standing between two large piles of food. The two piles are absolutely identical in size and content. The food looks delicious and attractive to the donkey. However, the donkey has a problem. Which pile should it eat first? The donkey examines one pile and then the other – they are both the same distance from the donkey so that doesn't help the equation. The next picture is of the donkey collapsed upon the ground between the two piles of food. In continuing to eye up the piles of food the donkey has, in the meantime, starved to death.

"Master what good shall I do to inherit eternal life?"
(Matthew 19:16)

Putting Love into Action

Unfortunately, many of us do not see prudence as a positive virtue – it has come to be seen as an excessive caution which refuses to take any risks. Rather like the donkey which cannot make a decision and thus consigns itself to a slow death, a person who is 'prudent' is seen as one who refuses to face life with its choices and challenges. This is not what prudence is all about. It might be better to use discernment today rather than prudence. This virtue enables us to take our ideas of the moral life and apply them to the concrete situations of our daily life.

Most of us have, at some time, been in a classroom or lecture hall listening to an 'expert' who had a masterly understanding of their subject but who couldn't communicate that knowledge in a way that made sense to anyone else. There are religious people who know intellectually about the moral life, but, who, in their living, do not live the truths they proclaim. Without the ability to put into practice their knowledge these people disappoint those around them and they can also undermine the very truths they uphold. The virtue of prudence is essential for their lives and ours if we wish to witness to that fulness of life which Jesus offers us.

Prudence is not granted to us in some magical way – we acquire this virtue through experience and reflection. This is one virtue where we really have to use our brains! The encouraging thing is that any experience, whether positive or negative, can help us to develop our ability to choose wisely. Most of the great saints have endured periods of sin, conversion and turmoil through which they learnt how to truly live good lives. God offers us the very same help in our honest struggles.

Action Point

"The choice may have been mistaken, but choosing was not." These words from a song suggest that indecision can be more crippling than choosing (even badly). Do I often put off making decisions which eventually mean that situations are worse than they need be? What can I do in the future to change this pattern of behaviour?

"Two roads diverged in a wood, and I -
I took the one less travelled by,
and that has made all the difference."
(Robert Frost)

Is there a time in your life when you chose differently from the people around you? What consequences did this choice have. What can you learn from this experience in deciding which course of action to take in the future?

notes

Justice

THE WORLD AROUND US: A recent report highlighted the fact that there are now more illiterate people in the world today than there were thirty years ago. Despite our advancing technology and belief in the 'progress of humankind' there are members of the human family who still do not share the very basic rights which we take for granted.

Walking through the streets of any major city it is hard to avoid the attentions of beggars – 'spare any change mate?' Meanwhile the latest headlines announce that the founder of company X is now worth ninety billion dollars.

Is Doing Justice an Optional Extra?

There is no doubt that we live in a highly complex and rapidly changing world. Yet, this should not permit us to close our eyes and say "I don't understand what is happening so can't really do anything." As followers of the Lord Jesus we are called to be people who actively seek justice – we are sent as apostles of the dignity and rights of each human person and community. "Blessed are those who hunger and thirst for righteousness, for they will be filled. Blessed are those who are persecuted for righteousness' sake, for theirs is the kingdom of heaven." (Matthew 19:6,10)

The Christian command to love is not simply a feel-good affair. Just as we often need tough-love in order to grow so does our society need a people who are tough-lovers – unafraid to stand up for those who are shunted to the edges of society or ignored altogether. Justice is one of the cardinal or ruling virtues – without a true sense of the immense dignity of each human being our love will not truly be active.

The Church looks at the virtue of justice in three different ways: agreements and arrangements between people; the distribution of resources, money and power between people; and, the basic needs of people (social justice).

In our dealings with one another we are called upon to be fair. When we enter into a contract then we should abide by its terms. However, if we are employers then the onus is upon us to ensure that the contracts offered are reasonable and that we also stick to the terms of the contract. The Church does not reject the fruits of

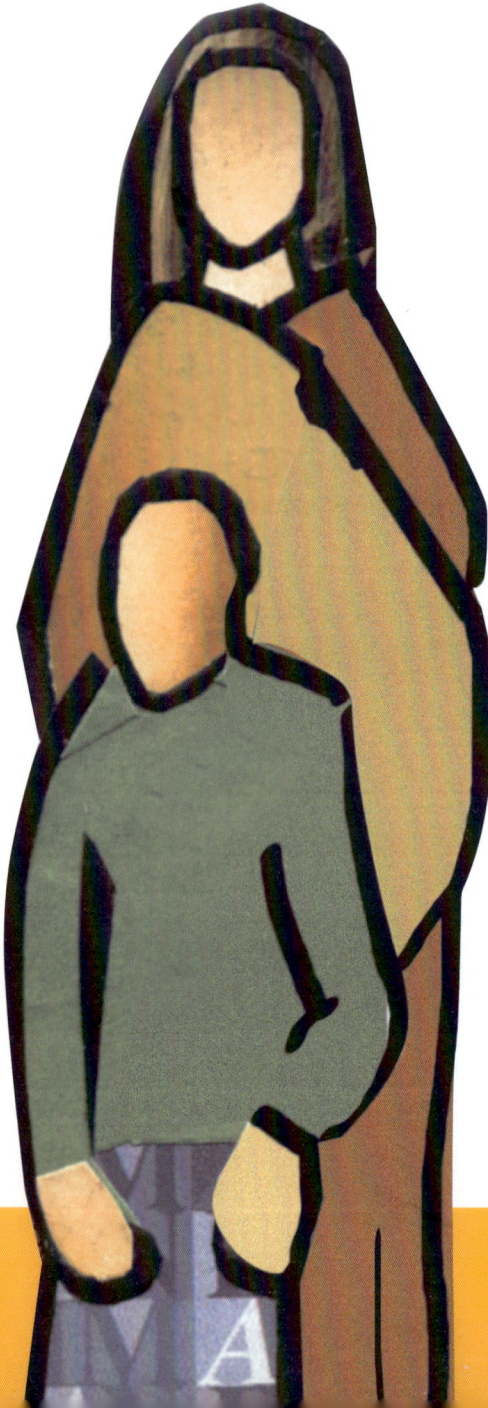

"Blessed are those who hunger and thirst for righteousness, for they will be filled. Blessed are those who are persecuted for righteousness' sake, for theirs is the kingdom of heaven."

(Matthew 19:6,10)

Action Point

Take time to really look at the stories in your own local or national newspaper. Are there stories describing situations of injustice? Are words used in a way that respects people and their rights or demeans them?

At work, at college, at home or in church, are there any people that are being treated unjustly? What action are you prepared to take on their behalf?

If you already give to charities consider finding out more about their work and how you might help them in non-financial ways.

For further reflection see the document produced by the Bishops of England and Wales, "The Common Good".

hard-work – but there should be an awareness of how resources are allocated – how much does the Managing Director of a firm get paid relative to the 'average' worker? These are important elements of ensuring that resources, wealth or power are distributed in a fair way. Are there individuals or groups of people who have been socially excluded? It is the concern of social justice to ensure that all people have the opportunity to contribute to society and be supported by society.

To practise the virtue of justice we need to develop our ability to see the world around us. Looking at the situations we find ourselves in we must then judge if the rights and dignities of people are being upheld and nurtured. Then we must act when we perceive any injustice and work for the building up of God's kingdom of love, peace and justice.

notes

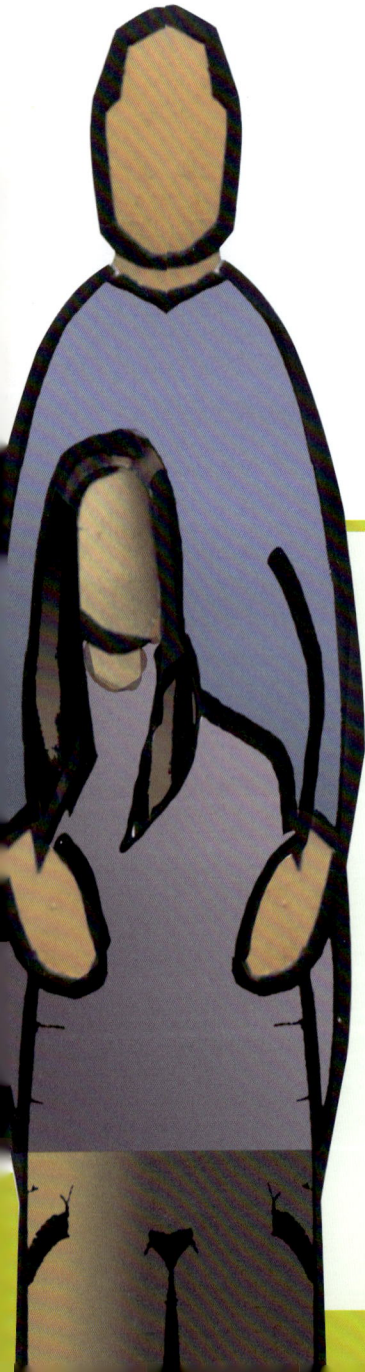

Fortitude

OUR GREATEST FEAR: A survey tried to discover the greatest sources of fear that people have today. There were some pretty unsurprising entries – fear of dying (no.1!), fear of heights, fear of failure, etc. However, there was one entry which we might not have really thought about before: at position number two in the top-ten list of fears was... the fear of public speaking. Indeed, a large number of people ranked fear of speaking in public as even more terrifying than death!

"My Father, if it is possible, let this cup pass from me; yet not what I want but what you want."

(Matthew 26:39)

notes
_____
_____
_____
_____
_____
_____
_____
_____
_____

Being Courageous

Martin Luther King was a pastor whose name we might never heard. Ghandi was a lawyer, how many lawyers have achieved international acclaim? How does Oscar Romero, a safe conservative bishop, find himself gunned down during Mass? What enabled these people to make a difference to the world and people around them?

A million-and-one people may have similar ideas about the situations of the world or the relationships that surround us. Yet, it is only those who act who make a real lasting contribution. They are people who overcome the fear or indifference which afflicts the crowd and step out onto the public stage willing to face the consequences.

The moral life is a life lived in public view – while our moral ideas and values may not be known to everyone, our action or inaction is clearly known. Fortitude, or courage, is an essential virtue in the character of anyone who is a follower of the Lord Jesus. If fear dominates our life then it does not seem likely that we can ever be truly effective witnesses to the Gospel.

We see in Jesus what it means to be a person of courage. Throughout his ministry he sees the needs of the people around them and acts to bring them comfort and healing. He does this even although he knows it will bring him into conflict with the religious leaders. His life of compassion and concern for all people leads to his eventual crucifixion. Jesus was aware of the consequences of his words and his actions. In the garden of Gethsemane his fear is real but it is not as strong as his love for the Father – this enabled him to continue to proclaim the Good News of God's love even to the very moment of his extermination.

When we live courageously we may not face martyrdom in a dramatic way. Yet it will cost us to leave our fears behind. Yet, each and every time we step out in faith and act we are drawn more and more into the freedom Christ's courage has won for us.

Action Point

"Cowards die many times before their deaths; The valiant never taste of death but once. Of all the wonders that I yet have heard, It seems to me most strange that men should fear; Seeing that death, a necessary end, Will come when it will come." Julius Caesar Act 2 Scene 2, 1.30

Are there areas of life in which you find yourself held back or bound by fear? Take time to list your main fears and try to split them into fears relating to God, to others and yourself.

Take your list of fears: for each one write down a simple step that could be taken to help overcome the fear. Take time to list the events, the people, the situations that really inspire you to act with confidence.

Share your fears with someone you trust and ask for their support in trying to face the future even more confidently and courageously.

Temperance

THE CATHEDRAL OF THE 20TH CENTURY: Just outside London is an enormous shopping centre, the largest in Europe. The walk right round the two-level complex lasts about 3 miles. There are hundreds of different shops: department stores; bookshops; clothes shops; stationers; newsagents; and a host of others. What is most distinctive about this shopping centre is the quality of its architecture and the numerous works of art throughout the building. There are large open spaces with beautiful sculptures, water features and shifting lights. To make sure that these are all enjoyed there are comfortable seats spread throughout the length and breadth of the mall. The designers of the shopping mall have included wonderful pieces of modern art work, have created zones in which to relax, have employed entertainers, for one purpose – to ensure that the visitor is relaxed and spends a long time in the centre and spends more money than they would do otherwise.

Temperance: A Healthy Self-Control

We live in a culture where we are contin-ually under pressure from other people, from companies, from the media, to behave in certain ways and to consume certain items. It can feel almost impossible not to be heavily influenced by all these voices. In today's climate the virtue of temperance is especially relevant.

Although the Temperance Society focussed on the refusal to drink alcohol the virtue of temperance has a much wider scope. Temperance is the virtue given so that each person can exercise some control over their compulsions and desires surrounding food, drink and sex. In many ways we can find ourselves behaving in inappropriate ways because of our need for physical satisfaction or comfort.

Christ reveals that the path to life and true freedom is found in self-control rather than in self-indulgence.

To live a life of healthy self-control we need, like Christ, to be aware of our true dignity and destiny in God. It is only by calling to mind how wonderfully we are made that we will be able to resist the illusions sold to us in the name of materialism.

Action Point

Traditionally, the virtue of temperance has applied to the areas of food, drink and sex. Take time to look at these three areas of your own life. What are the main struggles you face in eating and drinking healthily and moderately? What attitude do you have about your own body and sexuality? Are there habits in these areas which need to be brought under "control" to help you live life with more freedom and joy?

Are there any other areas of your life where it is difficult to maintain a healthy sense of control – shopping, over-spending, etc? Is there any simple action that you could take which would be the first step to taking charge of one of these areas?

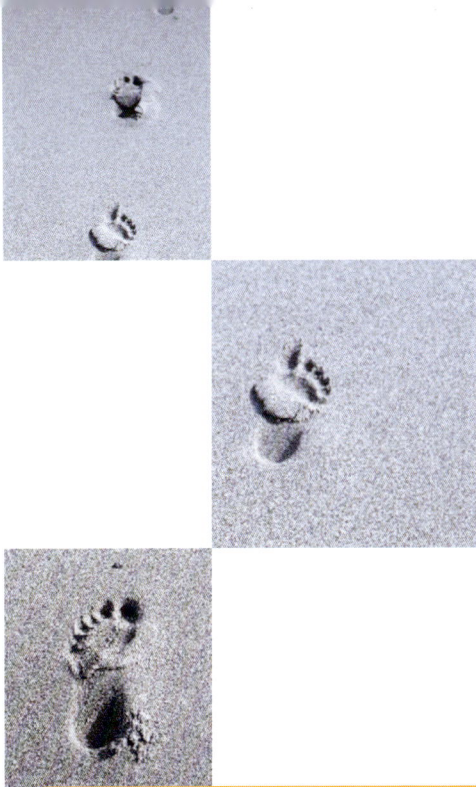

"The fruit of the spirit is love, joy, peace, patience, kindness, generosity, faithfulness, gentleness and self-control." (Galatians 5:22-23)

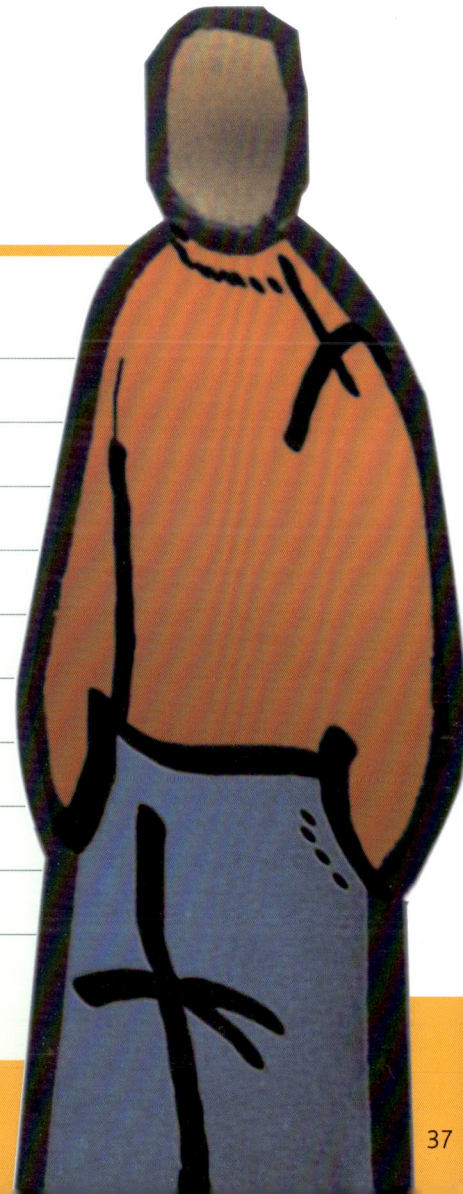

notes

Virtues are God's gifts

In the recent past many religious orders used to devote a month to the practice of a particular virtue, January was Fortitude, February was Temperance, etc. While useful in raising awareness of the virtues it also made them seem like things we could gain if we worked hard enough. We have spent time in these last few sections looking at our lives and the various virtues – we need to remember that it is God who enables us to grow in the virtues. As we focus on Christ and commit our lives to him it is God who will transform us through grace into images of his Son. We need to open our hearts to the Lord but it is the Lord himself who will form them for love and the Good Life.

Relationships

DOES THE CAMERA LIE?: The photograph had been well taken. The mood is one of relaxation. The characters in the picture are smiling gently. They are seated in a semi-circle at a table covered in a white cloth and bearing the remains of afternoon tea. The photograph shows four men and a woman. They are a wife and her husband, the husband's two brothers and a friend of the family. All five have enjoyed a warm friendship for as long as any of them can remember.

It is a happy scene. But what the photograph does not show are the day to day relationships within the group. It gives little hint of the personality of each person and of how they interact among themselves. The husband's two brothers run a small business against stiff competition and are constantly arguing about how to make it work. The wife's brother and her husband are alike in personality and deeply competitive with one another. If one says ' yes', then the other says 'no'. The friend of the family is a gentle sort of individual who will say or do anything for a quiet life. He is a man of few words and plentiful wisdom. The wife is a natural diplomat, able to restore peace when disagreements become too serious. All are committed Christians who have learnt to accept each other and who feel secure in each others company.

Relationships can be hard work

Relationships are not built by chance. We know from experience how much time and effort are required to maintain communication with others. In all spheres of life people need time to become familiar with one another. Relationships are fostered in the ordinary, informal course of day to day living. We might begin with the simplest greeting one day and, as the days go by, we move into conversation and social bridge-building. Relationship is the stuff of our human lives. People acknowledge each other through the spoken word, the tone of voice, gesture and the written word. Through relating each human being learns the value and importance of self. The baby gurgles and the parent gurgles back approvingly. Our ability to relate begins early as we grow physically and emotionally. Jesus himself has shown us the importance of relationship. He addresses us as his friends and invites us to stay close to him and to one another. In Jesus our relationship with one another challenges us to grow. Where love and respect abound we can feel secure enough to see our limitations and to work on them. We become mature.

Was it all different for Jesus?

As a major celebrity Jesus experienced the crush of the crowd during his tour of teaching and healing. In the midst of all the jostling he becomes aware of a special touch. A woman with an incurable condition had simply touched his cloak in the sure faith that she would be healed. Her faith was vindicated. The startling fact is that, in the press of the crowd, Jesus had felt power going out of him to that one person, and wanted to speak to her. This incident is recorded in the eighth chapter of Luke's gospel. One of the things it shows us is that Jesus likes to relate. The woman had related to him in her limited way and was rewarded. Through speech and touch they had related. In Jesus, relationship is our way to healing and growth.

Action Plan
Pray for someone whose personality
irritates you. Then spend a little time
talking to that person.

notes
_____
_____
_____
_____
_____
_____
_____
_____
_____
_____

Family

THE HOLIDAY: Two sisters planned the holiday of a lifetime for their husbands, their children and themselves. The holiday would take them to another continent where they would stay with other family members and their children. The preparations for the holiday were fraught with worries about missing the flight, saving money and having enough changes of clothing for the warmer climate. But they pressed on with their preparations, determined to give their children an unforgettable holiday. Ten months later the two families arrived tired and triumphant at the faraway home of their relatives. Two weeks of unfamiliar culture and new discoveries lay ahead. The visiting children and their many cousins became a small army that had to be fed and watched over. The adults' energies were consumed by the need to keep a protective eye on the youngsters, who enjoyed a carefree holiday. Back home after the holiday the two sisters and their husbands talked about the holiday and realised how much hard work it had all been because of the children. Did they have regrets, then? On the contrary, they were so pleased to have seen their children happy, boisterous, and content. It had indeed been well-worth the sacrifice.

notes

Will love change everything?

Love makes sacrifices and makes family life in all its forms possible. In the midst of the many pressures and challenges faced by parents and guardians of children that love is needed all the time. A sudden illness can strike down a family member. A spouse or other helper can depart or die. The one person earning an income for the household could lose that precious job. The pressures are with us constantly. A Christian family is not spared the challenges that face all families, but is called by Christ to follow him fully and deliberately. We sometimes hear of Christ as the unseen guest at the family table. In reality he is fully present in the committed loving relationships of the family members. His presence, through their faith, makes this a holy family. It does not make it perfect, but holy. Perfect families do not exist, but loving families do. A lone parent with children makes a family because Christ is here. Two families become a new family when the mother of one marries the father of the other. Christ is there to help both groups grow in love. Many of us see ourselves as members of an extended family. The presence of adopted members, of aunts and uncles, of grandparents and family friends enriches our experience of family life. All our families are loved by God.

What does the Bible say?

He was out of his mind. At least that is what people told the family of Jesus. This moment is recorded for us in the third chapter of Mark's gospel. But Jesus was perfectly sane and busily teaching the crowds and healing. He was in a crowded house when he got word that his anxious family was asking for him. He used the occasion to show that his family was now extended and made up of all who did the will of God. Mary, of course, is the first and greatest of this new family. She joined her whole life to that of Jesus, from the moment of his conception to the hour of his death. John's gospel records Mary's advice for all of us: 'Do whatever he tells you'

Action Plan

Is there a family member with whom you've had no contact for some time ? Write a long letter packed with family news.

Money

A MOMENTO: The loss was discovered the following morning and the owner was distraught. The cross and chain had been given to him as a child by his mother. It provided the most enduring link with her since her death many years before. He almost ransacked the house in his search for the precious object, but to no avail. Neither could he find it at his place of work. His friends promised to keep a lookout but, as the days passed, there was no sign of it. After a week he had almost abandoned hope when a chance encounter brought him face to face with his beloved cross and chain. Another parishioner was wearing it, having found it on the pavement outside the parish church. When the man asked for his cross and chain the other replied: 'Something for something.' This parishioner came from a tradition where any kind of loss was unbearable. He had formed a strong attachment to the cross and felt cheated at the thought of giving it even to its rightful owner. The matter was resolved by the gift of a prayer book while cross and owner were reunited. Being an understanding person the rightful owner had appreciated the power of attachment.

notes

Keeping a balance

We become attached to that which pleases us or helps us to feel secure. The attachment can be to people, places or things. We can become attached even to ideas and habits of thinking. To be human is to have attachments. But undue attachment to money is not good for us. Money is good and necessary for us as we need to buy food, clothing, shelter, recreation, transport, medication, and many other important things that help make living possible. Without money our modern developed economy would not exist. But an excessive desire for money creates problems for a Christian. This is because we recognise that Jesus is our Lord and we follow him. He teaches us how to be fully human and free. With Jesus as the centre of our lives we can judge the true worth of everything including money. But when we become unduly attached to money for its own sake we push Jesus from the centre of our lives and put a false god in his place. We become dominated by something which should be simply useful. A close attachment to Jesus and a healthy appreciation of the usefulness of money helps us to see that, in the end, all we have comes from God.

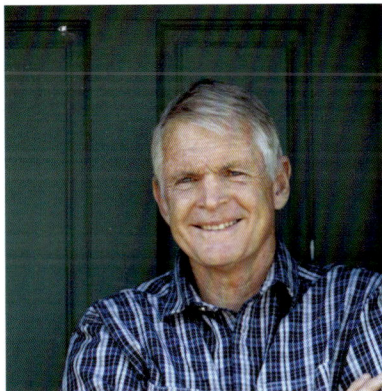

Where is our greatest wealth?

The man was rich and shameless, sporting the best clothing and daily devouring the finest food. At his gate lay another man, diseased and starving, to whom he did not give a thought. This parable is found in Luke's gospel, in chapter sixteen. The rich man's sin did not lay in his wealth, but in his attitude to God and to his stricken neighbour. By worshipping his wealth he had excluded both God and his neighbour. He was self-centred, indifferent and inhumane. Rich and powerful, he should have turned to God with thanksgiving and to his neighbour with pity. The rich man did neither and lost God forever. Our greatest wealth on earth is our relationship with God and with one another.

Action Plan

Identify a charity that you would strongly like to support. Then for one year give a weekly donation.

The Media

A local newspaper carried the story of a man whose fellow-worker had accused him of stealing. The police had been contacted by the employer and were investigating the case. In the meantime the man had been suspended from his duties. The incident made front page news and was accompanied by a photograph of the accused man. A young teenage girl and her father were discussing the article. The father expressed shock and dismay that the man, whom he knew, could have been so dishonest. Why did he do it? Surely he knew that he would be found out? And so the father's train of comment went on. The teenager was shocked also, but not at the newspaper story. She was amazed that her father could jump to conclusions about the man. She asked: 'But how do you know that he actually did it?'. Her father replied simply: 'It says so in the newspaper'. Holding up the newspaper she pointed to the word 'allegation'. This, she pointed out, is what the police are investigating. Four days later the same newspaper reported that the allegation had been false and that the man had been reinstated at work. The girl had applied her mind to reading the newspaper, while her father had read without thinking.

The power of words

Being able to read opens up for us a world of information, entertainment and many ways to earn an income. For this reason modern education gives great emphasis to literacy as a human right. As we journey through our education we come to appreciate the power of words. A word carefully chosen can have a great impact. Advertisers know well the power of the word as they pour out a torrent of messages through television, newspapers, radio, magazines and the Internet. They want to persuade us of their point of view. Everything we read and hear is presented from a point of view, including the news. In the face of so much persuasion what must the disciples of Jesus do and think? They rejoice in the world in which they live, simply because it is God's world. This is the world into which God sent his Word made flesh, Jesus Christ. Jesus is God's word of truth spoken to all humanity. With our minds firmly planted in God's word we are able to judge the value of every message coming to us through the mass media. Television, radio, the printed word and the Internet are good things because they help to connect people. They are sometimes abused but remain good. The Christian mind is never afraid of the media but willing to engage with them in the name of Christ.

What are the words God uses?

How shall we love God? Jesus tells us: 'You shall love the Lord your God with all your heart, and with all your soul, and with all your mind, and with all your strength'. This teaching is found in the twelfth chapter of Mark's gospel. It is clear that we love God with all that we are, and we see that this includes our minds. The human intellect is a wonderful gift to be enjoyed and exercised. In the Letter to the Romans, chapter twelve, Paul tells us to let our minds be thoroughly renewed by Christ. We give glory to God by applying our minds to all that we hear, see and experience, including the media.

Action Plan
This week read a longer article from the newspaper. Note how it is slanted and the kind of words used in it. Write your own comment on the article.

notes

_____

_____

_____

_____

_____

_____

_____

_____

_____

Politics

Tom was an excellent all-round handyman employed by the county council. He worked hard and was dedicated to the welfare of his young family. He and his wife had no particular political inclinations but tended to vote for the local independent candidate. Tom did have, however, a simple and direct view of politics in general. "Politics", he would say, "is the business of politicians. My business is to earn a living for my family". While reading the newspaper he would quickly pass over the political news to get to the sports pages to check out the horses and the football. A crisis catapulted Tom to centre stage in local politics. The county council was preparing to cut jobs during a time of financial difficulty. With his job in jeopardy Tom was invited by local activists to take part in demonstrations and to gather petitions. He gave up his free time for the sake of the cause. He found himself strangely belligerent as he questioned his local councillor about the forthcoming job losses and threatened to campaign against her at the next local elections. Sadly, the cause was lost and the redundancies went ahead. Although Tom's job survived he was now a different person. He had found his political voice.

Where are your political roots?

Politics is an important part of our being human and involves challenges and conflict. To be Christian is to be human, and to be human is to have opinions and a viewpoint. We should feel free to express our views and be able to appreciate the viewpoint of another. We do not have to agree, but at least be willing to give each other the courtesy of listening. We are all political in the widest sense in that we all have ideas about how things should be run and organised. This is true whether we think about the country, the borough, the parish, or our own small group. Whatever the level of involvement Christians belong in politics. They represent Christ in every situation: in the polling booth, the trades union, the centre of government. They may even find themselves in opposing political parties debating their differences with intelligence and vigour. But they remain rooted in Christ, accepting each other as sisters and brothers. Our vocation is to be rooted in Christ from whom we draw life and in whose name we act. We elect representatives to parliament but remember that we are all representatives of Christ.

The nature of leadership

"Is nothing sacred?", a saying which we often hear when someone behaves in an outrageous manner. The question could easily be put to some of those who were the chosen companions of Jesus, as we can see from the following incident. It is recorded for us in the twenty-second chapter of Luke's gospel. They were at the Last Supper and Jesus had just given them the gift of his body and blood. At this sacred moment the disciples debated among themselves as to which of them should be regarded as the greatest. It drew for them a compelling lesson from Jesus on the true nature of leadership. The incident shows us that, where people gather, there is politics. Under the leadership of Jesus we can always resolve conflict in a truthful and generous manner.

Action Plan

Be a witness to a council debate at the town hall.

notes

Our Parish

The parish church of St.Luke's is situated on a busy, fume-ridden road in a deprived area of the inner city. The celebration of Mass is frequently drowned out by the sounds of buses and lorries braking to a halt at the traffic lights just outside the door. The membership of the parish reflects the varied cultures and ethnic groupings of the district. Immigrants come to this church looking for solace and hope. The people here do not disappoint them. Over the years the parishioners of St. Luke's have worked hard to create a united community in the midst of their diversity. Not so far away is the parish church of Holy Trinity situated in a wealthy suburb of the same city. The streets are lined with mature trees and high hedges. During the celebration of Mass no distracting noise invades the church. Occasional bird song from the trees outside helps the prayer of the worshippers. There is an air of generosity here. The financial status of the parish is very healthy enabling the parishioners to support many needy causes.

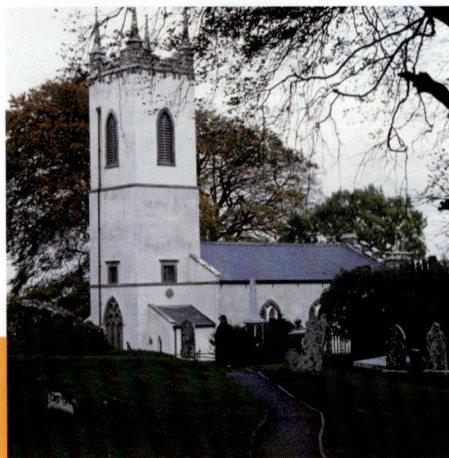

All parishes are the same and all parishes are different...

It has been said that all families are the same but different. The saying emphasises the fact that they have much in common while having important individual differences. The saying can be applied to parishes, which have in common their membership of God's family, their community life around the Eucharist and the Word of God, and a mission from Jesus Christ to promote his Gospel. What makes each parish different from other parishes is the unique mix of the people in it and the kind of area in which it exists. Parishes exist in real places among real people and each parish will find its own way of making Jesus and his Gospel known. Some parishes are financially better off and will have more resources for their mission.

But all parishes are wealthy in their members. Human beings are the greatest wealth in any parish. In a good parish the members are always ready and willing to appreciate and accept each others gifts. In every parish there are only first-class members. The Spirit of God lives in and works through each one to foster unity and growth. Each parishioner, regardless of health, sex, age, race or culture, is anointed by the Holy Spirit for the work of the Gospel. Each parishioner is a gift to the parish.

Who do we condemn in our parish family?

Condemnation was expected as the woman stood there in full view of everyone. Her crime was that of adultery and the penalty death. Would Jesus condemn her? On his word her life now depended. We read about this incident in the eighth chapter of John's gospel. Rather than condemn the woman, Jesus challenged the entire group about their own sins. His message to the woman was clear: 'I do not condemn you; avoid sin.' This triumph of the love of God offers us a pattern for all relationships in our parish. We begin by remembering that no one is without fault. If we want our parish life to work and thrive it is better for us to seek the best in each person. Appreciation helps us to grow and it draws the best from us. We must thank God for the high standard set by Jesus.

Action Plan

Write down the name of each parishioner who is involved in a parish group or ministry. Pray for each one lovingly.

notes

Life

In 1978 a salt mine in Eastern Europe was placed on the World Heritage List in recognition of its status as a wonder of the world. Over a time-span of seven hundred years many generations of miners had excavated over seven million cubic metres of salt. This "grey gold", as it became known, had brought in a healthy revenue for successive governments in that region. Throughout the centuries the fame of the mine spread beyond the country itself. The salt-miners were respected all over Europe, while eminent people who visited the mine reported on its spectacular beauty. During those same centuries other things were happening in the mines. A way of life developed that centred on mutual support and on deep faith in God. The miners created a sick bay two hundred metres underground besides chapels for prayer and the celebration of Mass. The miners had created a life-giving community hundreds of metres beneath the surface of the earth. While exploiting the mine they had preserved it, making it beautiful. In this most unpromising environment the miners did not simply exist, but lived and thrived.

"I thank you for the wonder of my being, for the wonder of all your creation."

Human rights – Human responsibilities

The drive to live is one of the most powerful forces in the world. It is a gift that human beings have in common with all living things. Life is God's supreme gift to all his creatures. To be alive is to be able to praise and glorify God. We are amazed by wonderful television programmes that reveal to us the complexities and richness of life on earth. We can now witness living things thriving in the most hostile environments. God loves all his creatures, but our human lives have a special place in his concerns. God created us for a conscious relationship with him through faith. It is no secret of course that the lives of many thousands are rendered unbearable by oppression and deprivation. They are oppressed by illness, disabilities, and prejudices about age, sex or race. Their lives are often undervalued by others. Yet they are human beings who have a right to be supported and respected and to be able to exercise their abilities. Today, happily, there is a great sense of the importance of human rights, and of the need for worldwide co-operation to make them a reality. Today we also see a growing appreciation of our dependency on the life and health of our planet. We do not exist in isolation from other life, but are dependent upon it for our food, medicine, shelter and clothing. In God's scheme of things human beings are stewards of creation, that is, they are gentle and respectful carers.

The nature of Creation

The book of Genesis tells us that God took a walk in the Garden, obviously at home in his creation. In other parts of the Bible we read of creation responding to God by offering him praise and worship. Indeed this is a vocation which human beings share with the rest of creation.
In one of the psalms the writer experiences a sense of awe at his own existence and that of all creation. In psalm one hundred and thirty eight, as used in the Prayer of the Church, we share the writer's sense of awe as he prays: "I thank you for the wonder of my being, for the wonder of all your creation."

Action Plan

Think about the earth and your dependence upon it. Spend time giving thanks to God for it and for your own place in it.

notes

_____

_____

_____

_____

_____

_____

_____

_____

_____

_____

Justice

A time-span of four years separates the two photographs. The same child appears in both pictures, first at age five, then as a nine-year old. Something has changed: in the second photograph she sports a radiant fresh-faced smile. Something had happened in the meantime. The first photo captured in her five-year old face the hopelessness of the whole family. Her family, like tens of thousands of others in her country, were landless peasants without a future and without hope. Their fortunes changed when the family gained rights to disused farmland which they had occupied, together with two thousand other families, on the day that the first picture had been taken. With her parents and brothers and sisters she now enjoys a modest security. Something else has given her cause to smile. She is learning to read and write in basic school buildings built by the families and the teachers. She loves school and boasts that she can now write her name. The amenities are a very long way from the ideal. They are too hot in the summer and too cold in the winter. Yet for the family and their neighbours it is all a wonderful achievement, with the school symbolising their hope for a better future. In this place the young pupils are taught their importance and value as human beings. It is right and just that they should learn this.

Who is my neighbour?

During the Preface of the Mass the assembled people of God declares that it is right to give God thanks and praise. Apart from it being right to praise God we all have particular reasons to do so. Perhaps we are blessed with good health and enjoy financial security for ourselves and our families. We give thanks to God for the education enjoyed by our children. Many good practical reasons will come to mind for giving thanks and praise to God. Quite simply we live in the right place at the right time, and we have the basics for life. This is not the case for countless numbers of our fellow humans. Newspapers and television flood our living-rooms with images of destitution, social injustices and political inequalities. The followers of Jesus respond in two ways to these injustices. In the first place we offer immediate help according to our means and circumstances. Then, secondly, we ask why these things are happening. Political leaders who support, permit or create injustices do not like being asked, "Why?". This question puts them uncomfortably in the spotlight of public opinion. It puts them under pressure. Christians are the voice of the voice-less. We speak out because God is affronted by injustice. We recognise that there is no-one who is not our neighbour.

A response to the lawyer

The lawyer demanded a definition of "neighbour". Jesus did not define the word but told a story. He gave a description of himself and his followers in the parable of the Good Samaritan. You will find this story in chapter ten of Luke's gospel. In this parable the Samaritan acts out of compassion. He recognises a fellow-human's dire need. At the end of the parable Jesus tells us to act in the same way.

Action Plan

Join your local Justice & Peace Group. If the group does not exist, why not help found one?

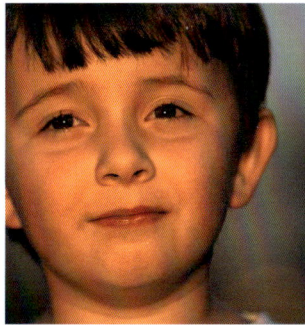

notes

The Church in the home

LET ME TELL YOU ABOUT THE TIME... John was a rather unusual young boy. It never really occurred to him to fight over the time he was supposed to go to bed. Nor did he cause chaos after the light was switched off and it was time for sleep. To what cause could this miracle be attributed? To the telling of stories – for each night, either John's Mum or Dad, sometimes both, would take time to sit on the bed and tell stories to John. "John, let me tell you about the time ..." Dark castles became places of light when invaded by the handsome prince. The beautiful princess could free the weary traveller with kindness and forgiveness transforming the traveller into a compassionate King. And then there were the strange and magnificent stories about Jesus, Paul, Moses and that amazing one about the man in the lion's den. John sat down on the edge of the bed. Now it was his turn. He looked at his daughter Amanda lying in bed and eager for the next instalment. "Amanda, let me tell you about the time..."

notes

Introducing One Another to Jesus

"One of these two who became followers of Jesus after hearing what John had said was Andrew, the brother of Simon Peter. Early next morning, Andrew met his brother and said to him, 'We have found the Messiah' – which means the Christ – and he took Simon to Jesus." (John 1:40-41)

Introductions can be so difficult. Walking into a room full of strangers and having to mingle can be immensely stressful for many people. Even those who appear super-confident can have a million butterflies in their stomach as they shake hands. Yet the moment of meeting is crucial – how many times have we missed out on a friendship with someone who could have shared our interests, our passions, or transformed our lives because we were never properly introduced?

It is in the home above all that we have the opportunity to be introduced to the life of faith and to the person of Jesus Christ in whom we put our faith. It is in the home that each of us have the opportunity to introduce one another to Jesus and encourage each other on the road of faith. Andrew seized the moment and took Simon to meet Jesus. We are encouraged to have the same enthusiasm and zeal in encouraging others to meet the Lord who is life.

With our words we draw a picture of God and with our actions we bring that portrait to life. It is said wisely that "Faith is not taught, it is caught". A believer cannot help but introduce others to God, the real question is, what kind of God are we introducing people to? A God of fire and judgement, a God of disinterest, or the living God revealed in Jesus Christ? We are always telling stories to one another throughout our lives, may we, like Andrew, like John speaking to Amanda, inspire others to faith by our telling.

Action Plan

Take time to reflect on the stories which you tell the people around you about God? What do your words and actions say about your relationship with God? Will this attract others to God or put them off? Ask the Lord to inspire you and to help you as you invite others to trust in him.

Have you ever told the stories about Jesus to your children, your grandchildren, your brothers or sisters? Do you have a favourite story from the Gospels? How would you tell this in your own words to someone you know?

The Church proclaims

RULES, RULES, RULES: In ancient India there was a great teacher named Guru Sunda. He taught everyone about living and dying. He would eat with the lower castes and the outcasts. Often he would find himself surrounded by hordes of sick people – he would reach out to them with compassion and they would go away whole. Out of love for the Guru his followers were determined to keep his memory alive – they wanted everyone to know how wise and compassionate he had been and to understand his profound teaching. So they sat down and wrote down all they could remember about him. Their stories and his teachings were collected into great and beautiful books which became the sacred texts for this new movement.

Each generation was introduced to the Guru Sunda through the sacred texts and were taught how to live as he had instructed through his wise teachings. But there was trouble ahead. The leaders began to become very protective of the sacred texts and began to keep them from the ordinary people – the people could no longer meet the Guru through the stories and the teachings he had once given. Then the leaders decided to simplify the Guru's message into a series of rules which people could follow.

Over the centuries the leaders multiplied the rules which members of the movement had to follow – to keep the movement pure, of course. But, one day a young child shattered the dreary peace of the people. Sneaking around the chief leader's palace he discovered a secret room in which he read the sacred text of Guru Sunda. Later that night he began to tell stories from the book to his family and friends – they marvelled at this man and his wisdom and his compassion – "Why has no-one ever told us of the Guru", they cried, "We have been burdened for years by rule upon rule but now we see that before the rule was the heart, the heart of Guru Sunda. Let us get to know him, that he may guide us anew."

"...united in Christ and guided by the Holy Spirit, press onwards towards the kingdom of the Father and are bearers of a message of salvation intended for all."

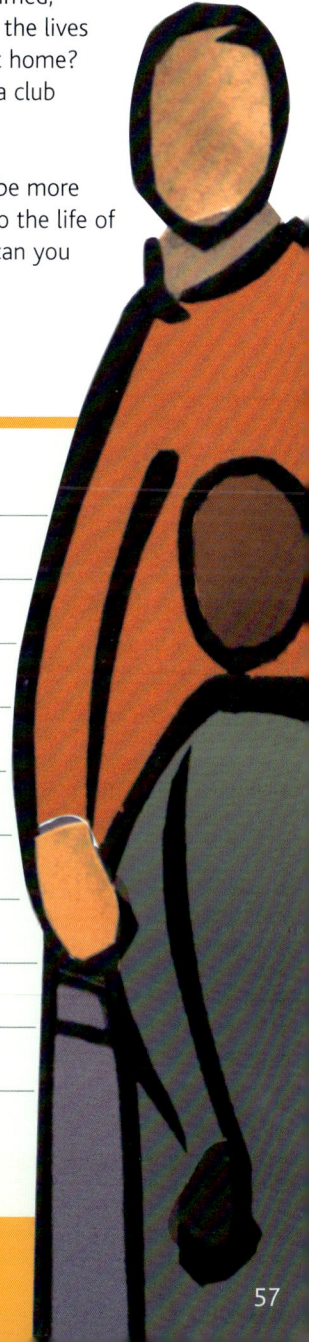

Sadly, for many people, the Church is identified with morality, with rules and with structure. Without the proclamation of Jesus these become burdens rather than life-giving. The one we proclaim is not simply a great teacher. The one we proclaim is Jesus the Christ, who offers a relationship of love to each and every human being – for this to happen we, as his followers, must know and proclaim him.

Action Plan

Take some time to reflect on the life of your parish. What is the life-giving centre of your parish? Would it be the Bingo, the CWL, the Parish Council? Or would it be the person of Christ as proclaimed, celebrated and worshipped in the lives of the people gathered and at home? Could the Church be seen as a club just like any other?

How can the person of Jesus be more central to your own life and to the life of your own community? How can you proclaim Jesus today?

Where is the heart of it all?

Paul, the super-apostle, is in the heart of Athens (see Acts 17). On each and every occasion he seizes the chance to proclaim God – God revealed in the life, dying and rising of Jesus Christ. This is his first task – to lead others to put their trust in the "name of the Lord Jesus". In Athens he did not meet with much success, but this did not stop him from proclaiming the Lord Jesus. This was Paul's first task and it is the first task of the Church and its members – "for theirs is a community... (who,) united in Christ and guided by the Holy Spirit, press onwards towards the kingdom of the Father and are bearers of a message of salvation intended for all." (Gaudium et Spes 1)

notes

The Church is seen

BACKPACKING INTO DANGER: "James spends twenty-three hours and forty minutes of each day alone in a cell containing a bed, bucket, Bible and Missal. James is twenty-six and is languishing in Kengtung Pison in Burma. What brought him here? He is not a drug-smuggler or organised criminal – he is something much more threatening – a pro-democracy campaigner. While backpacking in New Zealand he heard stories from Burmese refugees of the horrendous situation in their country. He decided to investigate himself and sneaked into the country. There he witnessed burning villages and mass graves. He was also arrested and deported. Returning to the country in 1998 he was arrested again after distributing pro-democracy leaflets and sentenced to five years in prison (after enduring eight days of torture). He was released after 99 days in solitary confinement having suffered from scabies, ear infections and insect bites."

Until recently he was in prison again – this time for "illegal entry and sedition" with a sentence of seventeen years. Shortly before returning to Burma he wrote: "Yes it is hell adjusting to Insein, (the prison he had been in) but I will not be languishing. I will be using every ounce of my wit and my strength to bring forward issues of human rights, and I will be in the perfect place to do it. I want to understand the junta, and I want the junta to understand the spirit of freedom."

"Very simply, not my will, but His Will: not my strength, but His strength: "Though I walk through the valley of the shadow of death, I will fear no evil, for Thou art my Rock, my Refuge." Then there is nothing to fear. But if I were to turn my back on my sisters and brothers as they were tortured and raped and murdered, then I would be ashamed and indeed I would fear. They are not only my family, they are your family too."

"Why do you call me 'Lord, Lord' and not do what I say?"

(Luke 6:46)

More information: www.burmacampaign.org.uk

Message

The Church, the community of the disciples of Jesus Christ, is seen in action in the lives of each and every one of its members. The Church need make no particular effort to be seen in the world today – it already is! Each action or inaction is witness to the message we proclaim. This brings difficulties – how can the Church proclaim the person of Jesus and the dignity of human beings and yet seemingly stand idle while injustice rages?

In people like James Mawdsley we find the answer. The Church is acting. Individuals and groups of believers are engaged in a proclamation by deed rather than word. The challenge facing all of us is to ensure that there is no division between our spiritual life and the rest of our existence. In the past the Church has backed up its teaching with actions in many ways – hospitals, schools, organisations to assist the poor. In praying "Lord, Lord" people found energy and resources to transform the lives of many people. Jesus invites us to do the same – may we who pray, may we who say "Lord, Lord", also be the ones who do the Will of the Father.

Action Plan

Take time to read and reflect upon Luke 6:46-49. Are there areas of your life where your words and actions are not matching one another? Is there one specific area where you can undertake something simple that will enable you to be a more effective witness for the Gospel. Pray for the courage to act confidently so that God's Kingdom may be glimpsed in your life.

notes

The Church listens

FAWLTY LISTENING: In the classic BBC sitcom Fawlty Towers there is a wonderful character named Manuel. Manuel is a Spanish waiter who attempts to work under the chaotic management of Basil Fawlty. Some episodes see Manuel come to warn "Senor Fawlty" of some imminent catastrophe. However, Basil never pays any attention to Manuel's pleas for attention. In fact he usually ends up being shouted at, man-handled out of the room, kicked or hit by Basil. Then we sit back and watch. Throughout the episode we watch Basil as he tries to cope with all the horrendous consequences of not listening to Manuel. Complication heaps upon complication as each and every person who crosses Basil's path is victim of his frustrated rudeness. Then, near the end, there is usually a scene where Basil Fawlty is utterly exasperated and asks, "Why didn't anyone tell me!" At this point Manuel skulks out of the room disheartened.

A simple conversation

When Jesus met the Samaritan Woman at Jacob's Well (John 4) he entered into a very simple conversation beginning with a request for some water. Then, gradually, the woman reveals more of herself to the stranger and Jesus begins to reveal the truth about herself and the Father's love. In doing this Jesus breaks the taboos that surrounded the contact between Jews and Samaritans, and Samaritan women in particular. In reaching out to listen to the woman he opens up a whole new life to her. The scene ends with the woman rushing back to her people and saying

"Come and see a man who has told me everything I ever did." She meets Jesus bound in painful relationships and leaves free to evangelise others.

As members of the Church, as communities, we are challenged by the life of Jesus to take seriously the lives and the stories of the people around us. We are invited not simply to ,'talk at' them but to enter into a true conversation. Very often, in these situations our own vulnerability will open doors to freedom for other people just as Jesus need for water heralded the woman's transformation.

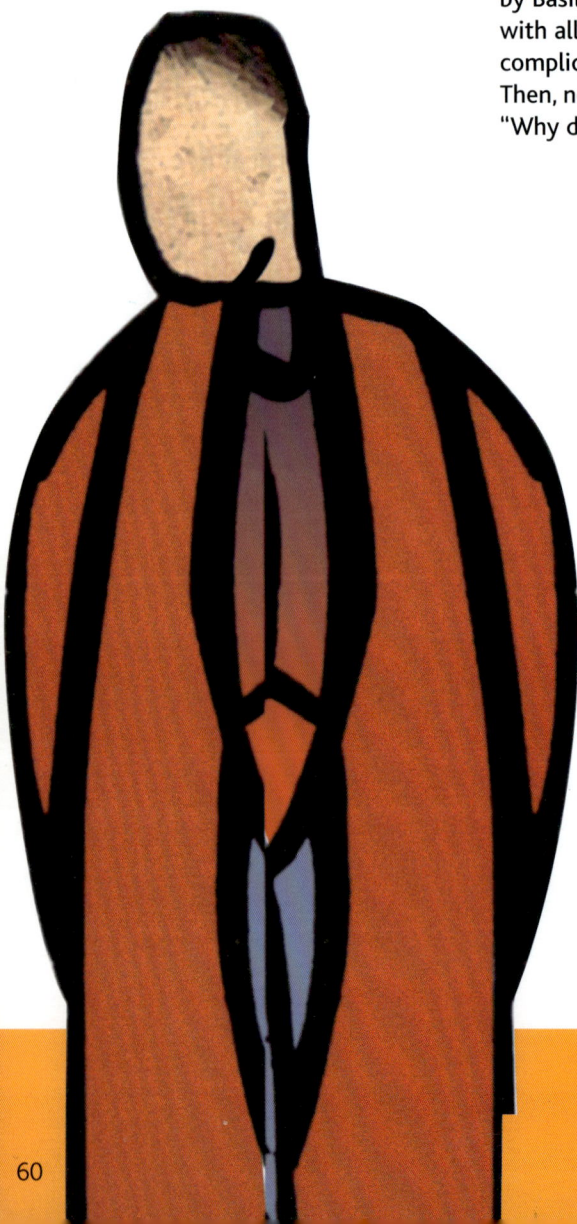

Take time to observe how the people around you communicate. Who are good listeners, who are not so good at listening? What makes the difference? How good a listener are you? While difficult to do, perhaps you might ask some of the people who know you well how good you are at listening. Is there something simple that you can do to help improve your ability to listen well? Perhaps you might like to try and simply listen (not talk) for a whole morning.

"I've just spent an hour talking to Tallulah for a few minutes." Fred Keating

By listening first we will allow ourselves to truly appreciate the need and the wonder of the people we meet. Then, when we speak, our words will be words of understanding not of judgement, words of hope, not despair, words of peace, not fear. The Church faces this task in our modern world. Church leaders need to engage in this process of true dialogue, however, for most people the life-changing experience of a listening Church will be their time spent with us individually. "The joy and hope, the grief and anguish of the men of our time, especially of those who are poor or afflicted in any way, are the joy and hope, the grief and anguish of the followers of Christ as well. Nothing that is genuinely human fails to find an echo in their hearts" (Gaudium et Spes -1)

notes

The Church Suffers

CHOOSING OUR BURDENS: High in the Alps two monks were making their way back to their Abbey. They knew that the weather was going to get worse and that they needed to be home before the worst of the snow-storms arrived. While making their way along a very narrow part of the path they heard muffled cries for help from down below in the ravine.

Peering down they could see a man who had fallen and obviously hurt himself – "Help me", he cried. The younger monk looked at the darkening sky and the terrible storm-clouds approaching and said, "This man has sinned, God has led him to his fate, now he must face the consequences of his life. Let us hurry home." The other monk was deeply saddened. "God has led us to this place that we may help him – we must rescue him."

But the first monk would not help and rushed off on his way back to the Abbey. The old monk made his way down to the bottom of the ravine and managed to secure the exhausted man to his back using some rope he had with him. Struggling with his burden he climbed up the steep sides of the ravine and began to make his way along the path. By this time the snow had begun to fall very heavily and it began to swirl around them as they made their way along. Eventually the snow became almost blinding and lay about four feet deep. Just as the monk spotted the lights of the Abbey ahead of him he tripped over something in the snow. Feeling around in the snow his hand found the frozen body of the young monk. Many years later a young novice asked the monk, "Master, what is the most difficult thing for anyone in life?" Remembering, he sighed and said," To have no burden to carry."

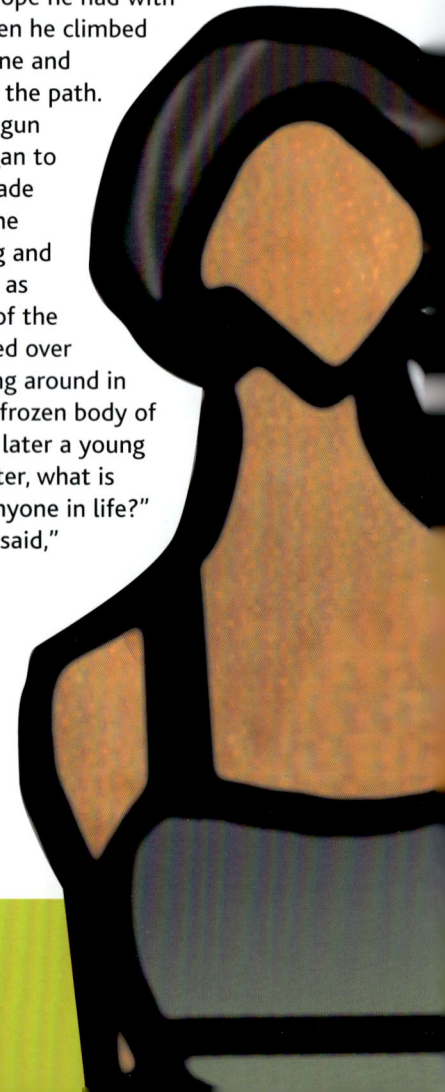

notes

_____
_____
_____
_____
_____
_____
_____
_____
_____
_____

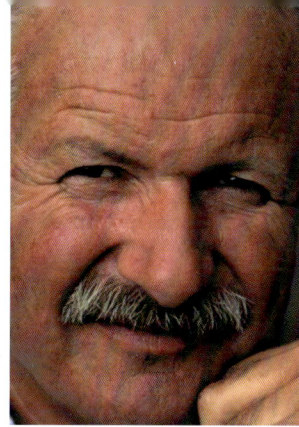

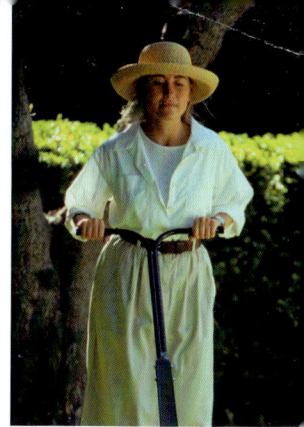

The mystery of suffering

"But we, we thought of him as someone punished, struck by God, and brought low. Yet he was pierced through for our faults, crushed for our sins. On him lies a punishment that brings us peace, and through his wounds we are healed."
(Isaiah 53:4-5)

Suffering is one of the greatest mysteries we face. There are no easy answers to the horrendous suffering we see in our world. Yet, the followers of Jesus know that suffering and pain do not have the final word. The redemptive suffering of Jesus offers us a way of life that transforms pain and death into healing and resurrection.

As a community it is not our job to condemn or to act coldly based upon our judgements. It is our God-given responsibility to reach out in all situations and to all people with compassion and active assistance. It is by living in this way that we remain close to the heart of Jesus and remain truly alive in the power of the Spirit. Often this will mean that others are dismissive of us, ridicule our actions or even oppose us directly – the suffering that we endure in these situations will transform ourselves and others with the power of the love of Christ.

Action Plan

Take time to reflect upon your life and the experiences of suffering which you have gone through. Have they been moments of growth and transformation? Have you ever suffered because of the help you have given to another or because of a stance you have taken? Is there someone you know whom you admire for their courage and ability to suffer for the sake of love?

Is there a situation of need near you that you have been avoiding because of the pain it may involve? Are you prepared to become involved? Do you need some help to do this – perhaps some other members of your community or some friends may help.

The Church Heals

"I'M SPECIAL": Jeanette was notorious.
Everyone in the parish knew her.
She was always at Mass each Sunday
with her (usually very fraught) Mother.
No-one ever knew what she would be up to
next – interrupting the homily with some loud and
inappropriate remarks – skipping or tearing around the aisles – holding onto a collection basket and fighting the usher for it! Everyone knew that Jeanette had special needs at school and home but they only had so much patience. After one particularly disruptive episode Mum and Jeanette were making their way out of church. The Parish Priest looked at Jeanette and asked Mum if it was okay for him to ask Jeanette something.

Mum was horrified, "She's overstepped the mark, I'm very sorry Father." Jeanette sat down with the priest at the back of the Church and they spoke for a few minutes. When she came out Jeanette was smiling – a huge smile from ear to ear. She had been asked if she would like to do a special job — to become an altar server. Mum wasn't sure but knew that Father John was aware of what he was letting himself in for.

Over the next few months Jeanette served regularly and everyone could see the transformation – was the graceful and reverent server the one-and-only Jeanette? Not only did she learn to serve magnificently, Mum began to notice lots of small changes at home. One day she asked Jeanette what had happened – "Mum, you are always telling me how special I am and how special I am to God. Now I know that I am special because God has given me a special job to do."

Healing is everyone's responsibility?

Even a quick look through the Gospels would reveal that Jesus spent a huge amount of his ministry engaged in healing – the sick, the sinner, the outcast. Jesus gave this ministry to his Church to continue in the power of the Holy Spirit. This is not just for saints with miraculous powers or people with "gifts of healing". All of us together are called to be a community of healing, offering wholeness of mind, body and spirit.

The Gerasene demoniac (Mark 5) finds himself, after his encounter with Jesus, "clothed and in his right mind".

As we, the community of Christ, affirm in word and deed the dignity and responsibility of each person, the healing love of Christ is poured out. As we welcome into our community and embrace with love the sick, the sinner, the outcast, we also are healed of the fear and hatred which keeps many entrapped.

Healing does not appear, or life truly thrive, where people are merely tolerated or allowed to exist. Jeanette experienced the healing power of love through the invitation to serve and be a full and active member of the community.

Action Plan

In your own life when have you experienced the healing power of another's love?
Has the Church brought you healing, if so, through whom was this channelled? If not, can you think of any way in which you will make sure that the Church is a healing experience for others in the future?

One of the most crippling effects of sickness in whatever form is the isolation that often accompanies the disease itself. Is there anyone you are aware of who is lonely and isolated, can you reach out to them – possibly with other members of the community?

notes

The Church moves on

One day Brian got into his car as usual and began to make his way along Canal Street and indicated left to turn into Station Road. He turned left, but couldn't help feel that something had changed. Shrugging his shoulders he carried on along the road and then flashed his headlights furiously at a car coming towards him on the wrong side of the road – the other car swerved out of his way and Brian carried on his way to work.

"All I can say is that I forget the past and I strain ahead for what is to come; I am racing for the finish, for the prize to which God calls us upwards to receive in Christ Jesus. We who are called 'perfect' must all think in this way." (Philippians 3:13-16)

Brian continued to turn left into Station Road each morning but became increasingly frustrated by the "crazy drivers" who were insisting on driving on the wrong side of the road. One day a visitor to the town who was driving along Station Road was surprised when Brian's car turned into the Road right in front of him. On went the brakes but to no avail. Brian was irate and demanded to know why the other driver was so stupid and driving on the wrong side of the road. "But this is a one-way street, " replied the visitor pointing to the signs which Brian had never noticed over the last month. "This can't be the wrong way to come – I've always come this way," cried Brian.